R.A.P.I.D. AUTOMATIONS

The 5 Simple Steps to Building Fast and Efficient Excel-Based Processes, Even if You Have Zero Tech Skills!

By:

Arjun Brara

Speed isn't the only thing the grind causes you to lose.

When was the last time you made a small oversight on something, or allowed 'human error' to creep in

There isn't anyone on the planet who could do a manual process over a thousand times, and not have "human error" creep in... (It's a part of being human)

If you've ever been told by a developer that a process automation will take millions in budget and 6 months in build time, to get an automated black box that no-one else understands...

If you've ever been told that any repeatable spreadsheet-based process cannot be automated

If you've ever been told there's no avoiding the manual handle-turning that's just "part of your job"...

You're in the right place.

This book is designed to teach you one thing.

How anyone can very quickly build automations that run efficiently, without needing anything more complicated than simply Excel, or any professional developer skills whatsoever.

First, we're going to cover what makes a process incredibly efficient, so what you automate can run as fast as possible.

We're going to start by building you a dashboard that gives you actionable results as easily as your iPhone battery indicator!

Simple and effective - letting you know whether or not to take the action of charging, or not charging your iPhone.

Once we know the exact result we want to achieve, we'll run through finding the minimal possible set of inputs needed to get that result

Then, when the start and finish line are precisely mapped out, we're going to dive into how to get from point A to point B shockingly fast, using what I like to call "Leaky Pipeline Theory".

Rather than spending a huge amount of time perfecting each part of our pipeline in the initial build...

We'll do the bare minimum to get a basic prototype up and running

Something you can see and play around with.

Which we can then test this by getting water flowing through, and just focus on fixing the leaks!

Once we've run a few samples and test cases through, we'll start turning up the water pressure to help us build in bulletproof validations which won't ever let you fail!

And even stress test it by putting pressurised water, or acid down our pipe to see if it holds!

You'll learn the right way to build an efficient prototype from the start, so you don't end up automating inefficiencies at the end.

And finally, automating the entire thing quickly and easily, without needing an entire IT team to do it for you - and how to easily maintain the build so your process doesn't turn into a black box which no-one in your department can understand, maintain, or easily develop.

If you're a project manager, or non-technical manager, feel free to skip the technical coding sections. The value for you, will come from knowing what's possible with good process automation, and how you can ask a technical person to achieve it for you. How you can deliver an entire process run from end-to-end, with a full and complete automated solution for everything.

If you're a team or technical manager, I'll show you how you can automate every repeatable process you have in your team, saving both time and costs as well as eliminating rework, or the stress that can come from the possibility of discovering mistakes down the line.

If you're an employee, consultant or contractor, I'll show you how to do your job in a fraction of the time it would've taken you before, and get a hugely better and more accurate result in the process by leveraging your time and expertise, allowing you to do significantly more in less time!

I do usually try and keep my website up to date with my latest developments as well - 'arjunbrara.com'

By the end of this book, I can promise you, you will truly Excel at Automations!

REPORTING DASHBOARDS WITH ACTIONABLE ANSWERS

Good reporting dashboards are all around us in everyday life.

In fact, they help us make a lot of the decisions we make on a daily basis!

The very best dashboards are the ones that integrate so seamlessly and simply into our everyday lives, that we hardly notice them. And yet, we make many of our decisions based on them.

The bad dashboards, or the poorly built ones, are the ones we end up not using after a while to make decisions from.

The battery icon on your phone is my personal favourite example of an incredible dashboard.

Most people wouldn't think of this as a dashboard because it's so simple and basic, and it gives you so little information!

On some phones, it doesn't even have the percentage sign, it's just a green icon, or a red icon.

But this simplicity is exactly what makes it incredible, and truly in my opinion, the single best dashboard I've ever seen.

It gives you just enough information to let you decide whether or not to take the action of plugging your phone into the charger, or to just leave it be.

It doesn't give you a billion different things. It just gives you the info you need to decide what action to take next.

And that's the exact criteria any good dashboard should provide.

The best way to tell how useful a dashboard is, is to find out how often that dashboard drives your decisions. And I feel almost everyone can say the simple phone battery indicator drives at least one decision a day for them.

The same goes for your car dashboard, telling you if you should stop by a petrol station, or even a car garage! Telling you if you should slow down, or you can speed up a bit.

While a car can calculate a billion different things with all the complexity and computers inside it, it doesn't. It only gives you the minimum information you need to make the best decisions, and take the best actions for yourself.

The products and services in the world that try to help drive decisions, and don't follow these principles, get used less and less, and eventually get phased out - which is how you can tell they have poorly built dashboards.

People stop using them to drive their decisions…

In this chapter, I'm going to take my interpretation of the techniques used by almost every big company that sells any product or service that people use to drive any decisions.

And breakdown how you can use the exact same principles to build world-class dashboards that run so smoothly and effectively, you hardly know they're there, while seamlessly guiding you to your goals.

We're going to do this, by following this 3 step plan:

1. We'll start with going through the 'Triple A' Dashboard process, so you get a dashboard that's as useful as to you an iPhone battery indicator

2. Next, we'll cover the simplest way to visualise and see your data to get the result you want

3. Finally, we'll cover the best way to validate that result, so you know it's right!

The Triple A Dashboard Process

The first, and most important thing you can do, is to ensure you never start building your process from the beginning.

Always start from the end, with the end-user experience.

This ensures the end goal you're working towards, is the exact end goal you want to hit.

Some processes tend to start with the inputs, and try to map inputs to outputs which look useful.

This commonly leads to calculating a lot of extra things just because they can be calculated, giving you a process which runs much slower than it should, as it's calculating things you don't need, and confusing the purpose you want to use it for!

Secondly, this also leads to not thinking about other useful outputs which could help get the best result,

Simply because they weren't available from the first set of inputs!

Starting by marking the outputs you'd want in a perfect world, means that if one of them isn't available from the inputs…

You'll see that right away, and likely try to find another way to get it!

These are just some of the reasons it's crucial to begin at the end - with the output you want to create.

The best way to do this, is by using the 'AAA Dashboard' framework to design it from.

This is important as using this framework helps prevent the creation of an output which won't be used, and is built just because it seemed like a thing that could be calculated.

This solves a lot of the problems we might otherwise encounter down the line, before they become an issue!

Achieve - What result are you trying to achieve with this process

Actions - What actions can you take to help you achieve your goals, and what answers do you need to help you decide on those specific actions? (All answers must be able to drive an action!)

Ask - What questions do you have to ask to achieve those 'actionable answers'

It is important that only the answers which tell you what <u>actions</u> help <u>achieve</u> your goals go in this dashboard!

Maintaining this simplicity makes it more efficient, easier to debug and develop from, and easier to build future new features on!

Going about it in this way lets you identify key inputs which might be missing right at the start

And prevents the crucial results we want to look at from getting obscured, or lost in irrelevant data.

This is the exact same 3 step process which almost every major dashboard that you use on a daily basis has behind it.

Let's look at an example:

11

Achieve - I want to get to a location using my car in the fastest time possible

Actions - To achieve this, I could either drive straight, or drive to the petrol pump to get fuel to get there.

Ask - I need to ask if I comfortably have enough fuel to get there, and to a petrol pump again afterwards.

Note how the car dashboard doesn't show you every single metric it possibly can. It shows you just enough to let you answer the question, which let you take the right actions!

Same with the speedometer. It presents the data differently because the speed limit constantly changes, but it gives you the data you need to make a decision on whether to speed up or slow down.

Applying this same thinking to a financial product like mortgages, might look like the following:

Achieve - I want to achieve the most profitable pricing for mortgages.

Actions - To achieve this, I could either decrease mortgage rates to get more customers, or increase mortgage rates to make more money from customers.

Ask - I need to ask what interest rate, relative to current market conditions, creates the most profitable balance of increasing customers staying with us, and customers paying us more.

Following this simple framework will let you create the simple dashboards you need to find your next actions.

It won't always be completely clear cut however.

Sometimes we may need more information for making judgement calls, or validation checks on the data processed for this period.

This should also be covered, however only after the initial dashboard reporting vision has been fleshed out, as that's what we are drilling down on, or validating.

Data Visualisations

We build dashboards for one of two reasons:

- Strategic Dashboards for Making Defined Decisions: (e.g. Tracking KPIs for management actions - helping us to make a choice from a largely pre-set series of possible actions)

- Analytical Dashboards Making Undefined Decisions: (e.g. Identifying data trends which let us make decisions based on data insights)

Each can crossover, we usually know a lot of the possible decisions which can come from data trends, but the aim with those dashboard is to explore the data and apply judgement to check.

Similarly, strategic dashboards which usually track KPI style metrics can lead to previously undefined decisions where a KPI goes significantly outwidth expected boundaries, or where multiple KPIs show something which is incongruent with each other.

A strategic dashboard which is used for KPI style defined actions. Some examples are below:
  – What was our profit/loss from a specific product last quarter - so we whether or not it's still viable to sell next quarter

  – What is our most profitable product to date - so we know which product to put more focus on selling

  – Based on the rate of sales, are we likely to run out of stock of any of our items - so we know if we need to order more in

An analytical dashboard which explores data is used when you use a data collection to help decide on an action. Again, some examples are featured below:
  – A subway map - letting you decide what the fastest way to your chosen stop is

- Drilling down on the products/policyholders that feed into a company profitability metric to explore possible drivers of that profit

Figuring out which result you want is most important before starting building out the dashboard will make it easiest for us to build the most useful possible dashboard for our user.

In most cases, the answer will be to have one or more strategic dashboards that let management easily see the data

And have one or more analytical dashboards that let analysts help identify data trends, or answer more complex questions around the data from management.

Data Validations

The biggest cost in over 50% of departments today, is rework, or not getting things right the first time.

Beyond that, there's opportunity cost with the time lost which could have been spent building other awesome things

There's the reputational damage, employee morale dropping, customer confidence both external and other teams not believing in you

Getting things right the first time, can have a very strong long-term benefit

Ask these 3 questions:

- What are all the ways someone can identify if something isn't right?

- What are all the ways someone can check the result is correct?

- Is there anything you left off the list because you felt it couldn't be systemetised or automated? ;)

Key in validating data, is making sure it is easily comparable to previous reports where possible, through standardisation.

Remember, the truth is in the trend, the power is in the pattern!

ALIGNED INPUTS

T he most common thing I've seen slowing processes down is when people take all inputs they can get which they feel might help.

Then calculate every metric and analytic which they think may help them achieve the goal...

Consider the following short scenario:

"A policeman is at a crime scene on a motorbike, 72 miles from the station

His motorbike can travel at 80 miles per hour.

Another policeman is at the police station.

His car can travel at 60 miles per hour.

The policeman at the police station, jumps in his car, and drives as fast as he can to the crime scene.

The policeman at the crime scene jumps on his bike at the same time and heads to the police station.

When the two of them cross paths, who will be closer to the police station?"

...

Take a moment to pause here, and have a go at this.

See if you can solve it!

...

...

If you solved it, well done!

If not, you see it's not actually your fault... You've definitely got the ability to solve it. This question is phrased in a way that sets you up to fail.

And this question is far too reflective of many of the processes which currently exist in the world...

Let me ask you the exact same question, but phrased differently.

Let's analyse it using our RAPID method!

Let's start with the end goal, completely ignoring all the inputs we have available.

Our goal is to figure out the position of one policeman relevant to the other when they cross paths, so we know who is closer.

So what do we need to know to figure this out?

When the two policemen cross paths, how far away is one policeman to the other?

Do you need any of the initial inputs the question provided to answer that?

Do you even need any inputs at all to answer it!?

...

When they cross paths, they are of course equally distant from the police station by definition, and so no other inputs can serve any use other than to confuse us.

Just because inputs which seem like they could be useful are available, it doesn't mean they do anything to help us hit our goal.

This is the exact same with building a process.

This is why we always start with the reporting part of the process.

Now that we know what dashboard reporting we want, our goal in the second phase, is to get only the bare minimum inputs that directly align with we need to create that.

Any other inputs are useless. They just creates noise which distracts you

Any information you can't take action on is pointless to know, and simply wastes time and resource finding out

Only take what you need to get the answers you initially decided you needed, anything else should not be feeding in.

Pipeline - Building Your 'Leaky Pipeline'

Once you have the reporting views you're trying to get to, you know what you want to create, and you have the inputs you need to create them

The next stage is to build what I like to call a "Leaky Pipeline".

The best way to do this is to find a test case or a bunch of test cases. A bunch of cases where you know, given certain inputs, the right outputs you should be expecting from them, and then try and build a functional example that gets you there as fast as possible.

If you get to the end and everything is perfect for all 100% of scenarios, that's bad. It means you spent too long trying to build a perfect solution at the start.

You want to build a functional test case as fast as possible, that just gets the result for a couple of test cases that you lay out in advance.

Create a bad first draft just to rush it through.

Once you've got something kind-of functional, we can work on iteratively improving it.

Find the *"Leaks in Your Pipeline"*

By just focusing on fixing where the leaks appear, you can laser focus your time, and build things in the most efficient manner.

Breaking this down into simple steps:

1. Find simple 'Proof-of-Concept' test cases of known results from example inputs

2. Build the bare minimum to get the test cases functional

3. Test, and focus on fixing just where the process falls down

Excel is almost always the best tool to build things in because of it's flexibility, readability, and speed of build.

It's something everyone in your company will likely be familiar with, so can be easily understood and maintained.

Unless you need custom C++ for huge financial models, or have very large data sets you're trying to wrestle with, Excel and vba are the generally the best things to use for process builds.

When building spreadsheet processes, it's always important to try and ensure you're applying good spreadsheet practise right from the start.

80% of the result of good Excel building comes from a few small things, and the same goes for 80% of the results in VBA.

There's a million other things that get you the extra 20%, but the following few small levers, will get you 80% of the result almost every time.

Excel Build - Best Practice

For good Excel build, the key is to never repeat calculations.

If you do need to use a result, calculate it once and reference the result.

It's amazing how many things in Excel somebody can do without realizing they're doing the same calculation twice!

And so, this makes it a very easy trap to fall into.

Ones that are obvious that most people would pick up on are things like using an INDEX MATCH function. If you're using a MATCH function multiple times, always do the match outside of the data table, and then reference it.

Don't recalculate the MATCH in every single cell in a big data table. That's terrible spreadsheet practice, and an example of one of the worst things you can do in building Excel workbooks!

The next example, which slows workbooks down the most, which most people don't realize is calculation dimensions.

SUMPRODUCT is one of the most flexible and versatile functions in the world. However, with that flexibility and versatility also comes a massive speed hit.

SUMPRODUCT usually looks across two dimensions. It's an array function, and so it's aggregating across two dimensions for each cell if it's used in a big data table.

Every time it does a calculation, picking one column as an example, for the first cell in the column, it's doing aggregations across the backing columns.

Assuming that formula is copied down, it's doing those exact same aggregations for every single cell in that column. This is very inefficient.

The right way to do it is to have an intermediary table in between.

The intermediary table has the exact same number of rows, or the exact same number of columns as the initial data table, and just as the aggregations across rows or columns and the final table, which you want to get to instead of using a SUMPRODUCT, you can use a SUMIF function. SUMIF are always hugely faster than SUMPRODUCTS because they're only summing across one dimension.

If possible, try not to use SUMIFS at all. This looks like it is a lot faster because it seems like it's a SUMIF type of formula, but it's still doing a lookup multiple times.

24

The right way to do it is to concatenate all the fields you want to lookup into a single lookup key, and do a single SUMIF on that.

The place where SUMIF falls down is when referencing an external workbook. In that case, you kind of have to use SUMPRODUCT, if you want to use an external link and keep the same conditional summing functionality.

Either that or you can bring a copy of the underlying data through completely! This is usually the best option if the underlying data isn't too huge, as it lets you see everything used in the process all in one place.

Remember, simplicity is key for Excel formulae. The purpose of putting something in an Excel formulae as opposed to VBA is to make it simple and easy for the user to follow.

If you have huge formulae in Excel, this starts to defeat the purpose of putting it into Excel and you should look at seeing if that might be better placed in VBA, where someone can more easily add comments and structure. (Or break it out into multiple, smaller Excel formulae!)

Vlookup/HLookup/Match formulae are some of the most commonly used Excel formula, however these are also generally the most inefficient formula in any workbook!

This is especially true when the last argument is set to the default of "False", or 0, making the code search through each and every individual value in the list to try and search for your result.

If it's only searching for data a couple of times, it's generally ok, however, when you've got a list of 10,000 items, and each of them is looking up a table of 10,000 to match something, you've suddenly looking at 50 million calculations! And most of those calcs are repeating the same thing!

Assuming the data set affected is reasonable large and worth looking at, the first and most important thing, is to get rid of, is the inefficient default search algorithm which looks through everything, indicated by the 4th argument in the function, the "False".

Setting this to "True", turns it into a binary search function, which means the number of calculation needed are insane amounts smaller! A table of 10,000 values looking up 10,000 data points, changes from 50 million calcs, to about 300,000 calcs. The difference between those numbers only grows as the data size grows.

Now for the binary search to work, the data has to be sorted, otherwise it fails. If the data cannot be sorted, this method can't be used. And even then, if the data point doesn't exist, the binary search will point to the wrong value! And so, to account for this, we must replace the old vlookup, with 2 vlookups to speed it up!

As crazy as that sounds! Let me break down the example below:

Before:

=VLookUp(A1,data_table_01,3,False)

After

=If(\$A\$1=VLookUp(\$A\$1,data_table_01,1,True),VLookUp(\$A\$1,data_table_01,3,True),"#N/A")

The second formula first checks that the binary search returns the right result, then uses it. If not, it triggers whatever error condition was set by the user.

As long as you can alphabetically or numerically sort the data being looked up, this tweak will massively speed up your result!

Something else that should be considered, is switching this to an "Index/Match" function, especially if you're using more than 2 columns in your dataset.

VLookUp generally reads in data you aren't going to use, and does so both in big quantities, and repeatedly! Index/Match only takes in the data you're going to use, and shifts itself when you insert and delete rows or columns. Unless you've only got one column you're using, there is no benefit to using vlookup over Index/Match.

And of course, it goes without saying, the exact same is applicable to HLookUp formula!

Now ideally, these calcs shouldn't be done in Excel at all! However you look at it, whatever formula you use, every Excel based solution to this still involves taking in the entire data set you're looking up from scratch each and every time, repeating the exact same task, which is the definition of inefficient!

This is due to the nature of how cells exist in spreadsheets, each one is completely isolated from the others in terms of calcs.

This is a good example of a calc which is much better moved to VBA, as it doesn't have the same 'Memoryless' and independent properties which we have in Excel.

VBA Build - Best Practice

In VBA, 80% of slow or inefficient processes are always caused by too many interactions with Excel. This is the single biggest thing that slows down VBA code.

If your data stored in Excel, grab in one go with vba so only one interaction

Use below code as example

arrData = Sheet("Sheet 1").Range("A1:Z99")

Same for writing out to sheet

Below code as example

Sheet("Sheet 1").Range("A1:Z99") = arrData

Avoid things like "WorksheetFunction" as they use Excel functions to do things, as opposed to VBA.

Calculations are generally most efficient when done in VBA.

Some calculations can be orders of magnitude more efficient in VBA, due to the fact it can 'remember' previous calculations, whereas in Excel, each cell works completely independently of the others.

A good example of this, is the 'VLookup' formula we were looking at in the earlier section.

The absolute best way to tackle those sorts of problems, is to read in all the data through VBA, and store it in a VBA-Based Dictionary Object.

This would take 1000 data items from 1000 lookups (and close to a million Excel calcs!), down to just a few thousand VBA calcs! And would scale up for larger data sets similarly!

Below is a simple example of a dictionary object being used. (Note that "Microsoft Scripting Runtime" must be ticked under 'Tools -> References' for this to work!)

Imagine we are reading in a data table that looks like the following:

Key	Value
a	11
b	22
c	33
d	44

```
'Declare the New Dictionary Object
Dim dictData as New Dictionary

'Add the items to the dictionary
dictData.Add "a", 11
dictData.Add "b", 22
dictData.Add "c", 33
dictData.Add "d", 44

'Retrieve the value you want!
Msgbox dictData("c")
```

Note that for your automation, you would read the data in from a worksheet, or external source, and programmatically add it to the dictionary. Similarly with reading it out, it would go to a variable, and then get saved or stored somewhere as opposed to just a pop up.

I've just laid it out as above for demonstration purposes, to make it easier to follow the data flow, and understand so that you can easily incorporate it into your own process.

Building out Your Pipeline

The idea of building a leaky pipeline is making sure you get a functional example up as fast as possible.

Following these good practice steps will make sure you build that functional example in an efficient and easily extendable way.

Once you have your functional example for a few test cases up, you can start testing it on an entire data set. This is how you can start building up your leaky pipeline.

From a metaphorical term, I like to think of this as a pipeline that gets water from A to B. It's not going to be perfect because you've rushed to build it.

You've just try to do this as fast as possible. And you figure out whether or not it works by taking some water and pushing the water through the pipeline.

At the parts of the pipe where the water isn't leaking, you can see if those parts are good enough to hold the water to hold your data set. They don't need any more attention.

And even though you've rushed the build, you can see that it works and it gets you the results you're after and you've done it in a significantly reduced time.

The bits that don't work are going to have water leaking out of them. And because it's a pipeline, you can see exactly where those leaks are and focus your time and effort where you need to focus your time and effort without wasting time on things you don't need to waste time on.

Once you've done that, the next stage is turning up the water pressure, stress-testing it. What happens if someone puts a lot of data through but through a different data set, a data set that someone hasn't expected, putting high pressure water.

I like to think of this as putting high pressure water through the pipeline and seeing if the pipeline still holds.

Maybe some bits of the pipeline will hold for our functional examples or initial data sets. But once we start testing it with other more complex data sets, it falls apart.

But again, just like a pipeline, the parts where it falls apart are very obvious because we can see water squirting out of those parts and we can focus our time on only those parts without worrying about the rest of the pipeline.

Because while a pipeline isn't 100% absolutely perfect, it's perfect for the purposes of our data and everything we want to use the process for.

We can try stress-testing it afterwards by trying to break it. I like to think of this as pouring acid through the pipeline. We can see if we try to pour acid through the pipeline, is our pipeline strong enough to deal with it, to handle these errors, to handle things a user might try in the process.

Anywhere we see the acid leaking out of the pipe, we know that that's the bit of the pipe we have to reinforce. That's the bit of the pipe that wasn't built strong enough to withstand user error or any other type of error that crops up.

Note, that if you have a huge data set, Excel may not be the best tool for this. If you have files that are a gigabyte big, you could use some VBA to parse it and work through calculations.

However, that's the time where you could start looking at Microsoft Access or a different application, as Excel and VBA isn't typically built to handle this.

Same thing goes for any data set that's over roughly 100,000 rows. Excel can take up to a million rows, but that's designed for things like opening a CSV that's close to a million to be able to see the data.

It's not designed to have a processor that has multiple calculations sheets, each of them having a couple of 100,000 rows with like 100 columns each.

That will break the workbook or cause the workbook to become so big that it will crash very often and become almost functionally unusable.

Thoughts should always be given as to making sure Excel is the right tool for what you're trying to accomplish.

Once you passed all your test cases past your initial dataset test, done your stress-testing and your acid testing, you can comfortably see the pipeline is no longer leaky and will hold anything and everything you throw at it!

Integrity - Bulletproof Validations for Precision Perfect Results

The next stage in the RAPID process is integrity, bulletproof validations to know that you can always trust your outputs.

There's two types of errors you'll have to deal with in any process.

One is where the process fails halfway through and doesn't run to the end. It crashes.

Maybe it doesn't crash, and it flags up an error message to the user. Both these fit into our first category.

The second type is where there's an error somewhere in the process, but the process doesn't highlight this, doesn't stop, keeps running to the end, tells you everything is okay, when in reality it isn't.

The first error usually seems bad, but it's actually a very good type of error. That's the errors we want.

We want to stop the process or catch it or do something if something goes wrong, and make sure we catch it and give the user some useful information about it, and make sure we don't let anything through that could cause a wrong result without it plugging up.

Key to avoid this is making sure we avoid phrases that suppress all errors. In VBA for example, this is 'On Error Resume Next'. Other coding languages will have similar options.

'On Error Resume Next' means whatever error comes up, just ignore it and plow on. This is possibly the most dangerous phrase in coding, and shouldn't ever really be used when writing code.

For spreadsheet formulae like Excel, the equivalent is the IFERROR function. These can sometimes be useful if the fact something fails in general tells you something, but in general, IFERROR, and similar functions are definitely ones to try and avoid, as it can lead to the previously mentioned second type of error, where we get an end result that we believe is correct but isn't because an error that happened midway through the process got suppressed.

The first type of error is the one we want to watch out for and create meaningful error messages for the user if they come up. We try and trap all of these errors by thinking about

1. What are all the different possible things the end user could do that could break this process?

2. What are all the different data combinations that could come in that could break this process?

3. What other system interactions could happen that could break our process?

Once you have a complete list of all three of these things, then we create test cases around all three of them and test all of them.

That is sufficient to ensure that we have a very robust process with all the integrity checks we need to ensure the output is always what we expect.

DETACH - AUTOMATING IT ALL SO YOU CAN FOCUS ONLY ON YOUR AREA OF EXPERTISE

Finally, the last stage of the rapid process is detach. This is to detach the human completely from the workings of the process.

The process should ask if these are for the inputs, run automated to check those inputs are okay, and then from a command like a button click, the process should automatically generate the outputs without need for human interaction.

This is very important for two reasons. Not only is it the automation that helps speed everything up and make sure the user doesn't need to waste their valuable time on manual handle churning, having it automated means you can trust the outputs are definitely what you expect them to be because you've done only integrity checking beforehand.

This is why it's important to think of this more than just automation. It should be a complete detachment of human involvement from the process.

The last gem I'm going to leave you with, is something that proves anything can truly be automated - and shows you how you can write a macro that let's a blind person see!

(Colour blind that is!)

38

What if I told you VBA could create a virtual keyboard which presses keys the same as a human would, except without making typos and a massively increased keystroke speed?

What if I told you VBA would let you create a virtual mouse which you could programatically move around, and click the buttons the same as a human would, except with a computer's speed and precision?

The only 2 ways in which a human can interact with the computer is through the keyboard and mouse. Both of those things can be virtually emulated by creating an interface object for them in vba, and therefore can be fully controlled and automated!

This is the final piece of proof that any process can be truly automated.

Every way in which the human can interact with the machine can be fully replicated in a programmatic way.

It's very important to note this is always the absolutely worst way to automate anything - literally nothing can be worse! However, any form of automation is always better than manual! Not only for speed, but accuracy too.

Let's dive into the keyboard controller first.

Emulating keyboard keys is relatively simple. It just requires the following command:
Application.SendKeys "Text to Write", True

Where 'Text to Write' is whatever keys you want the computer to emulate. There are some special keys which require alternative commands instead of the relevant letter or number, these are listed below.

Key	Code
Backspace	{BS} or {BACKSPACE}
Break	{BREAK}
Caps Lock	{CAPSLOCK}
Clear	{CLEAR}
Del or Delete	{DEL} or {DELETE}
Down Arrow	{DOWN}
End	{END}
Enter	~ (tilde)
Enter (From Numeric Keypad)	{ENTER}
Esc	{ESC}
Help	{HELP}
Home	{HOME}
Ins	{INSERT}
Left Arrow	{LEFT}

Num Lock	{NUMLOCK}
Page Down	{PGDN}
Page Up	{PGUP}
Return	{RETURN}
Right Arrow	{RIGHT}
Scroll Lock	{SCROLLLOCK}
Tab	{TAB}
Up Arrow	{UP}
F1 to F15	{F1} to {F15}

If needed, you can use key combinations, for things like shortcuts where you hold down a specific key while pressing another.

Those keycodes are listed below

Key	Preceding Symbol
Shift	+
Ctrl	^
Alt	%

Virtually any key combination you would ever need to emulate can be done using some combination of the above.

The last thing we need to be able to emulate to cover all the ways a human could input anything to the computer, is the mouse!

To do this, we first need to put in place some Windows API calls for the mouse controls. The following 2 functions and 'Type' object, need to go at the top of your module, before you start creating any procedures or functions

Private Declare Function SetCursorPos Lib "user32" _
(ByVal x As Long, ByVal y As Long) As Long
Private Declare Function GetCursorPos Lib "user32" _
(lpPoint As POINTAPI) As Long
Private Type POINTAPI
x As Long
y As Long
End Type

The first function shown above 'SetCursorPos', is designed to set the position of the mouse cursor.

This can be called and used as shown in the following example

dummy_value = SetCursorPos(20,30)

The above function would move the mouse cursor to 20 pixels away from the left of the screen, and 30 pixels away from the top of the screen.

42

To get the current position of the cursor (allowing us to know how far to move it if we just want to move it, or if we want to check it has indeed moved there), we can use the following code

Dim a As POINTAPI
dummy_value = GetCursorPos(a)

This will return the position of the cursor as a 'POINTAPI' object called 'a', where the left and top component of it can be retrieved using the lines shown below

Debug.Print a.x
Debug.Print a.y

The above shows example where the values are printed to the console, however it would typically be used to read back into variables to be used further on in the procedure.

The mouse moving combined with the time delay can also be useful if you want to keep a machine active until a certain point at night in order to kick off a process which must be started overnight for maximum efficiency.

We can use these controls to write our macro that can can cure colour blindness for the purposes of any spreadsheet!

It all stems from the fact vba can be used to extract the pixel colour from the screen at the point the mouse is hovering over.

So, if someone is colour blind, we can create a macro triggered by a key combination, which after a few seconds delay (giving the person time to switch windows), the code will retrieve the colour of the pixel being pointed at.

It can then give the red, green, and blue component of the colour, as well as match up from a list of colours which colour descriptions come closest, to give them a more descriptive view of the colour!

Thereby, giving the previously colour blind person, the ability to tell the absolute exact colour of any pixel on the screen, and tell even better than someone could with a human eye!

We can retrieve the colour of a point on the screen as follows

```
'Declare all the Windows Functions
Private Declare Function GetPixel Lib "gdi32" (ByVal hdc
As Long, _
ByVal x As Long, ByVal y As Long) As Long
Private Declare Function GetCursorPos Lib "user32" _
(lpPoint As POINTAPI) As Long
Private Declare Function GetWindowDC Lib "user32"
(ByVal hwnd As Long) _
As Long

'Create a Cursor Reference Object
Private Type POINTAPI
x As Long
y As Long
```

End Type

```
'Convert to RGB Colour Code
Public Function ConvertToRbg(ByVal HexColor As String)
As String
    Dim Red As String
    Dim Green As String
    Dim Blue As String
    HexColor = Replace(HexColor, "#", "")
    Blue = Val("&H" & Mid(HexColor, 1, 2))
    Green = Val("&H" & Mid(HexColor, 3, 2))
    Red = Val("&H" & Mid(HexColor, 5, 2))
    ConvertToRbg = Red & "," & Green & "," & Blue
End Function


'Function to Retrieve the pixel colour
Function Get_Colour() As String
    Dim tPos As POINTAPI
    Dim sTmp$, lColour As Long, lDC As Long
    lDC = GetWindowDC(0)
    Call GetCursorPos(tPos)
    lColour = GetPixel(lDC, tPos.x, tPos.y)
    sTmp = Right$("000000" & Hex(lColour), 6)
    Caption = "R:" & Right$(sTmp, 2) & " G:" & _
    Mid$(sTmp, 3, 2) & " B:" & Left$(sTmp, 2)
    Get_Colour = ConvertToRbg(sTmp)
End Function
```

The above code in the function 'Get_Colour' will return the red, green, and blue component of the colour the cursor is currently pointed at.

VBA code can then be used to compare it to colours in a list with the red, green, and blue properties of each colour. An example with simple colour is shown below. This can be expanded to a more detailed and granular list, however this is most suitable for demonstration purposes.

HTML / CSS Name	Decimal Code (R,G,B)
Black	(0,0,0)
White	(255,255,255)
Red	(255,0,0)
Lime	(0,255,0)
Blue	(0,0,255)
Yellow	(255,255,0)
Cyan	(0,255,255)
Magenta	(255,0,255)
Silver	(192,192,192)
Grey	(128,128,128)
Maroon	(128,0,0)
Olive	(128,128,0)

Green	(0,128,0)
Purple	(128,0,128)
Teal	(0,128,128)
Navy	(0,0,128)

For each value in the table above, calculate the difference between it's red/green/blue component, and that of the colour being read in. Square all the differences, and get the square root of the total. The smaller the number, the closer the fit!

Where this fits into writing automations, is if we know a certain message pops up, or display changes somewhere, we can use vba to move the mouse there, and test the pixel colour of a specific place where we know which pixel colour represents that process being complete is, and which pixel colour that process not being complete is.

Simply use the mouse moving code from earlier, test the result of the function 'Get_Colour' from above to the target colour you want it to be.

If you're feeling adventurous, and you want to create a macro that spits out the closest matching colour name, you could get a more granular list of the above colours, get the code to match them all, output the list next to them, and sorted by the likelihood of it matching that value!

In fact, there's a hell of lot more you can now do!

Writing macros that can see for you is just the beginning...

CONCLUSION

The world is moving more and more towards trying to build automations and more efficient processes. By reading this book, you are already well ahead of the curve.

In addition to this book, I've created other resources to help you on your journey.

Something else I've built is an Excel web app!

I call it... Excelopedia!

http://arjunbrara.com/excelopedia

It solves the 2 most common Excel problems.

The First Most Common Problem - Your Excel formula doesn't work, or returns an error

We've all been there...

The worst is when it's a 23 line formula built by the last person to own the process

But never fear!

Type any Excel function into the search bar, and this web-app will give you a list of all the valid input which won't cause an error, the possible causes of errors for that function,

And if nothing else works, how best to debug that function.

The Second Most Common Problem - You want a formula to do something, but aren't sure what to use!

Just filter on the category of function you are looking for, and the app will give you a list of all the different functions relevant to what you are trying to do that could help you, and how you can use it!

And if you want to reach out for a personal consultation on any of this, or discuss me coming to your business to implement this for you

Feel free to get in touch through my website.

http://arjunbrara.com/

Thanks for reading,

Arjun